The Portfolio and Its Use

Developmentally Appropriate Assessment
of Young Children

The Portfolio and Its Use

Developmentally Appropriate Assessment of Young Children

CATHY GRACE
AND ELIZABETH F. SHORES

With
Mac H. Brown
Frances D. Arnold
Stephen B. Graves
Tom Jambor
and Monty Neill

SOUTHERN ASSOCIATION ON CHILDREN UNDER SIX

Little Rock, Arkansas

SACUS

Copyright © 1991 by Southern Association on Children Under Six
All rights reserved, including the right to reproduce this book or portions thereof
in any form, without written permission of the publisher.
Published by the Southern Association on Children Under Six
P.O. Box 5403, Little Rock, AR, 72215-5403.

Library of Congress Cataloging in Publication Data
Grace, Cathy and Elizabeth F. Shores
The portfolio and its use: developmentally appropriate assessment of young
children

First Edition
Designed by Elizabeth F. Shores
Printed in the United States of America

ISBN 0-942388-05-4

This manual is dedicated to the South's teachers and children and to the memory of Joseph H. Stevens, Jr., Ph.D.

Contents

Acknowledgements

Many persons contributed to this manual. Great credit is due to Mac H. Brown of the University of South Carolina, Frances D. Arnold of Auburn University at Montgomery (Alabama), Stephen B. Graves and Tom Jambor of the University of Alabama at Birmingham, and Monty Neill of FairTest for their contributions to the text of this work.

The Editorial Board of the Southern Association on Children Under Six guided the development of the book, helping us recognize a void in the literature on assessment and evaluation and plan how SACUS could fill it. The members of that board deserve mention here: Milly Cowles, chairwoman, Nancy Bacot, Joseph H. Stevens, Karen Robertson and John Johnston.

The Northwest Regional Educational Laboratory at Portland, Oregon generously allowed us to reproduce portions of *Assessment in Early Childhood Education; A Consumer's Guide.*

Teri Patrick of the University of Arkansas at Little Rock Children's Center provided longitudinal observations of several of her five-year-old students. This was not the first time that Ms. Patrick helped the staff of SACUS, and we are grateful for her support.

F. B. Johnson of Little Rock, Arkansas shot the photo illustrations in this book, donating his services as he has done many times before. Andy, Cherise, Sommer and Brandon Martini of North Little Rock and i. j. routen of Little Rock drew on their real-life experiences as parents, children, and teacher, respectively, to pose for those photographs.

Annie Webb of Little Rock proofread the galleys.

Finally, we must acknowledge the children whose drawings are reproduced here. Sasha Parrish of Montgomery, Alabama painted the rectangles on the cover. Other children at the Auburn University at Montgomery Early Childhood Education Center drew the pieces that illustrate the progressive acquisition of concepts. Artworks by Mason Grace and Layet Johnson, both of Little Rock, appear in the section about work samples.

Cathy Grace
Elizabeth F. Shores

August 29, 1991

The subject of children's achievement and performance, in school and even before they enter school, has received increasing public attention during the latter 1980s and early 1990s. Much of the discussion has seemed to ignore the natural development of children and the question of how achievement and performance of children should be measured or judged. Yet parents, teachers, school administrators and education policymakers hardly can support young children's eager efforts to learn if they themselves do not understand the ways in which children learn. Nor can they document children's progress if their testing methods do not relate to children's experiences.

Early in the present decade, President George Bush proclaimed that "by the year 2000, all children in America will start school ready to learn," coining a phrase that irked, distressed or amused early childhood educators who knew that, barring serious illness or disability, children are *born* ready to learn. At about the same time, the Southern Association on Children Under Six (SACUS) in 1990 released a position statement on developmentally appropriate assessment. The term *developmentally appropriate* refers to the standard that curriculum, instruction and assessment be appropriate to a learner's developmental level. Thus, it is developmentally appropriate to decorate the wall beside an infant's crib with black-and-white art, as the infant cannot see subtle pastel colors. SACUS recommended a ban of the routine, mass use of standardized intelligence, achievement, readiness and developmental screening tests for children who are eight years old or younger. This recommendation was based on the body of research that indicates that such children are not developmentally ready for such tests.

SACUS does recognize and endorse the important function of assessment in planning programs for young children. The association has established criteria for appropriate assessment of such children (SACUS, 1990):

Assessment must be *valid*. It must provide information related to the goals and objectives of a program.

Assessment must *encompass the whole child*. Programs must have goals and assessment procedures which relate to children's physical, social, emotional and mental development.

Assessment must involve *repeated observations*. Repeated observations help teachers find patterns of behavior and avoid quick decisions which may be based on unusual behavior by children.

Assessment must be *continuous* over time. Each child should be compared to his or her own individual course of development over time, rather than to average behavior for a group.

Assessment must use a *variety of methods*. Gathering a wide variety of information from different sources permits informed and professional decisions.

After the president proclaimed the National Education Goals, the National Governors Association appointed the National Education Goals Panel to monitor national and state-level progress toward the so-called readiness goal and others. The Panel in turn appointed a resource group to recommend specific steps for achieving the readiness goal. The resource group reported in March, 1991, that defining and measuring "readiness" would be difficult (Resource Group Interim Report, 1991). The group considered several techniques of assessing the performance and achievement of young children and recommended that, by 1995, all schools incorporate *observations by teachers* and *performance portfolios* in the assessment and evaluation of young children.

The use of portfolios as a means of assessing children is not new to the early childhood profession. Good programs for young children have always included multi-dimensional assessments of the children as a continuous part of curriculum review and development. Assessment of children's develoment and learning is absolutely necessary if teachers are to provide curriculum and instruction that is both age-appropriate and appropriate for individual children (NAEYC, 1991).

This manual explains and illustrates the use of portfolios as a viable and legitimate means of assessing young children. It is hoped that program administrators, teachers and parents who read this will agree that good alternatives to standardized tests exist — and that by beginning to use portfolios, they can transform bad practice into good.

It is also hoped that this manual will affirm those who already recognize the value of basing judgments of young children on the real accomplishments of those children, rather than on abstract data collected in isolation from their day-to-day lives.

References

National Association for the Education of Young Children and National Association of Early Childhood Specialists in State Departments of Education (1991). Guidelines for appropriate curriculum content and assessment in programs serving children ages 3 through 8. Washington, D.C.: NAEYC #725.
National Goals Panel Resource Group (1991). Interim report: Readiness for school. Washington, D.C.: National Governors Association.
Southern Association on Children Under Six (1990). Developmentally appropriate assessment. Little Rock, AR: Author.

Chapter 1

Why the Assessment Portfolio Should Be Used

Even before the president and the National Governors Association aimed the spotlight of government attention on American student achievement, testing, particularly of young children, had become controversial. In North Carolina, for example, opponents of standardized testing of young children waged a decade-long battle to stop the state's mandated standardized achievement testing of children in first and second grades. Finally in 1987 the North Carolina General Assembly directed that "the State Board of Education shall also adopt and provide to the local school administrative units developmentally appropriate individualized assessment instruments consistent with the Basic Education Program for the first and second grades, rather than standardized tests. Local school administrative units may use these assessment instruments ... for first and second grade students, and shall not use standardized tests" (General Assembly of North Carolina, Session 1987, House Bill 2641). This was the first successful statewide grassroots effort to stop the overuse and misuse of standardized tests and insist on appropriate assessment of young children.

While no other state has banned all standardized testing of young children, other Southern states have dropped requirements for testing young children, leaving assessment decisions to local governing bodies. Decisions to reject standardized testing of young children are the result of the limitations and dangers of these tests. They are limited because they fail to adequately measure the abilities and achievements which they are intended to measure. They can be dangerous because they encourage harmful education practices and because many children are erroneously sorted and labeled according to test scores (Medina and Neill, 1990; Ellwein, et al., 1991).

Focusing on testing means ignoring most of the curriculum and instruction that young children receive. It also means that *children are taught in the wrong way*. Instead of learning by doing, exploring, solving real problems and enjoying self-initiated activities and projects, children are supposed to learn by practicing for tests. This practice usually consists of ditto sheets, seat-work drill, and brain-numbing repetition. Ironically, after a decade in which "teaching to the test" came to dominate as a means of improving education, the U.S. school drop-out rate exceeds 30 percent in many states (Hodgkinson, 1991).

Those tests have also disempowered and deprofessionalized teachers, who are told that their judgments about the children in their classes are less valuable than the results of standardized tests. Younger teachers, who entered the profession after standardized tests became accepted practice, may know instinctively that test procedures which are so stressful they cause some first-graders to vomit from fear are inappropriate, but they may not know what the alterna-

Focusing on testing means that children are taught in the wrong way. Instead of learning by doing, exploring, solving real problems and enjoying self-initiated activities, they are expected to learn by practicing for tests.

tives are.

Teachers in preschool programs may not feel the same amount of pressure to use standardized tests. However, they typically are expected to prove the success of their teaching approaches by proving the progress of their pupils. In an attempt to provide "reliable" data to parents and administrators, some preschool teachers choose to use standardized tests, without considering compatibility between their curriculum goals and content, or whether their instructional methods relate to the format of the tests. Some preschool teachers work frantically to get children "ready" to prove themselves on upcoming kindergarten entry tests.

Standardized tests simply cannot meet the needs of individual schools, classrooms or children. They therefore are instructionally useless. Likewise, they provide limited, often misleading, information to the public. By contrast, other types of assessment and evaluation can help the teacher immediately improve instructional practice as well as provide useful information.

Northwest Regional Educational Laboratory (1991) lists several characteristics of appropriate assessment:

- •Measures multiple dimensions of child development
- •Is implemented as an ongoing process
- •Generates data useful for instructional improvement
- •Takes place in a natural setting

2

- Takes advantage of a variety of the child's natural response modes
- Provides information that can be shared with parents
- Is free of cultural or gender bias

The laboratory has reviewed a number of commercially-available assessment instruments according to these criteria. A summary of that review is reproduced as Appendix E.

Good assessment methods improve teaching and learning. They are an integral part of the curriculum and instruction in a developmentally appropriate classroom or program. They improve teaching and learning.

The assessment portfolio or process-folio is an excellent means to assess children as they move through the curriculum. It is a record of the child's process of learning: what she has learned and how she has gone about learning; how she thinks, questions, analyzes, synthesizes, produces, creates and interacts, intellectually, emotionally and socially, with others.

According to Meisels and Steele (1991), portfolios serve several important purposes, including:

- Helping to integrate instruction and assessment
- Providing students, teachers, parents, administrators and other decision-makers with essential information about children's progress and various classroom activities
- Enabling children to participate in assessing their own work
- Keeping track of individual children's progress
- Forming the basis for evaluating the quality of children's overall performance

This manual describes the components of the assessment portfolio as well as methods by which teachers can collect that information and material.

References

Ellwein, M.C., Walsh, D.J., Eads, G.M. and Miller, A. (1991). Using readiness tests to route kindergarten students and the snarled intersection of psychometrics, policy and practice. *Educational Evaluation and Policy Analysis*, (Vol. 13, No. 2), 159-175.

Hodgkinson, H. (1991). Reform versus reality. *Phi Delta Kappan*, Vol.73(No.1).

Medina, N. and Neill, M. (1990). *Fallout from the testing explosion*. Cambridge, MA: FairTest.

Meisels, S.J. and Steele, D.M (1991). *The early childhood portfolio collection process*. Ann Arbor, MI: Center for Human Growth and Development, University of Michigan.

National Association for the Education of Young Children and National Association of Early childhood Specialists in State Departments of Education (1991). *Guidelines for appropriate curriculum content and assessment in programs serving children ages 3 through 8*. Washington, D.C.: NAEYC, #725.

North Carolina Department of Public Instruction. (1987). Grades 1 and 2 assessment. Raleigh, N.C.: Author.

Northwest Regional Educational Laboratory (1991). *Alternative program evaluation ideas for early childhood education programs*. Portland, OR: Author.

Southern Association on Children Under Six (1990). Continuity of learning for four- to seven-year-old children; A position statement. Little Rock, AR: Author.

Chapter 2

Defining the Assessment Portfolio

Teachers should continually and thoroughly assess children's progress in order to maintain a developmentally appropriate program. As they note changes in children's skills and interests, they can adjust the program to further accommodate each growing child, for example by planning different activities for free-choice periods in the children's day. Using an assessment portfolio gives teachers and children flexibility in planning activities that will promote physical, affective, social, emotional and cognitive development.

The teacher's specific objectives will determine the extent to which she uses a portfolio. Some teachers regard portfolios as a useful part of assessment, while others find that portfolios are adequate by themselves for the assessment and evaluation of young children. In either case, portfolios should contain information from various sources which is collected systematically over time.

The following terms are used frequently in discussions of testing. (The abbreviation NAEYC refers to the National Association for the Education of Young Children.)

•*Assessment* — The process of observing, recording and otherwise documenting the work which children do and how they do it, as a basis for educational decisions which affect those children. Assessment can draw upon a variety of instruments and measurement strategies (NAEYC, 1991; Northwest Regional Educational Laboratory, 1991).

•*Evaluation* — The systematic collection and analysis of program related data that can be used to understand how a program delivers services or what the consequences of its services are for the participants (Northwest Regional Educational Laboratory, 1991).

•*Assessment Portfolio* — A collection of a child's work which demonstrates the child's efforts, progress and achievements over time. Accumulation of a portfolio involves the child and the teacher as they compile the materials, discuss them, and make instructional decisions (Meisels and Steele, 1991). It is a means of assessment that provides a complex and comprehensive view of student performance in context (Paulson, et al., 1991).

•*Readiness Test* — Assessment of a child's degree of preparedness for a specific academic or preacademic program (NAEYC, 1988). This is not considered an appropriate form of assessment of young children.

•*Standardized Test* — An instrument composed of empirically selected items that have definite instructions for use, adquately determined norms, and data of reliability and validity (NAEYC, 1988). This is not considered an appropriate form of assessment of young children.

•*Achievement Test* — A test that measures the extent to which a person has mastery over a certain body of information or possesses a certain skill after instruction has taken place (NAEYC, 1988). This is not considered an appropriate form of assessment of young children.

•*Intelligence Test* — A series of tasks yielding a score indicative of cognitive functioning (NAEYC, 1988). This is not considered an appropriate form of assessment of young children.

•*Screening Test* — A test used to identify children who may need special services. It focuses on the child's ability to acquire skills (NAEYC, 1988).

•*Anecdotal Records* — Brief narrative accounts of a child's behavior which are significant to the writer. Anecdotes describe incidents factually and objectively, recording how, when and where they happened. Teachers often write such accounts soon after the incidents occur (Beaty, 1990).

•*Rating Scales* — Tools that indicate the degree to which a person exhibits a certain trait or behavior (Beaty, 1990).

•*Work samples* — Examples of a child's work which have been saved as records of the child's progress (Carini, 1978).

•*Checklists* — Lists of specific traits or behaviors arranged in a logical order. As they observe children, teachers and parents can use checklists to note the presence or absence of those behaviors (Beaty, 1990).

•*Systematic Observation* — Regular, deliberate and thoughtful listening, watching and recording of a child's behavior.

Work Samples

Work samples are a major component of the assessment portfolio (Meisels & Steele, 1991). Examples of these samples are:

•Students' writing, drawing, number-writing, and problem-solving exercises
•Logs of books read by students and parents
•Photos of noteworthy block constructions
•Notes and comments by the child about her own work or activities
•Copies of pages of journals (with invented spelling preserved)
•Drawings or illustrations inspired by stories or music
•Tape recordings of children reading stories, both published ones and those they write or dictate themselves
•Stories which children dictate or write
•Video recordings of special projects, events or performances

Engel (1990) emphasizes that "work samples meet the need for accountability while recognizing and supporting individual progress." She calls this "keeping track" of a child's progress — in other words, following the child's success rather than his failure.

The teacher who keeps a loaded camera handy can easily photograph significant achievements, such as this child's tower. The teacher can note the date and other significant information about each photograph as she shoots it, in a small notebook stored with the camera.

An anecdotal record accompanying this photograph might note that the child erected two identical structures and commented, "These match!"

I was trapped in a cage. I will tell you who put me in here. The nasty forces of evil. The ghost threw me in this cage, but I got out. I found something. The floor was made of concrete, but I found an old concrete smasher. And I smashed it. It made a big hole.

Mason Grace

A teacher might choose to add a work sample to a child's portfolio because the child's use of several media reflects planning and an increased attention span. This drawing and dictated story appears on both sides of the paper. The child used pencil, pen and crayon and then cut out additional images and stapled them to the work. After transcribing the child's dictated story, the teacher noted the child's name and the date.

Michael Jordan is trying to do a slam dunk
and Todd Day is blocking his way.

Layet Johnson Aug. 13, 1991

When the teacher asked this five-year-old to "draw something you enjoyed this summer,"
the child recalled watching the National Basketball Association playoffs with his father.
His addition of Todd Day, a forward for the Arkansas Razorbacks, and a snarling dog
on a leash to the action demonstrate an interesting synthesis of reality and fantasy. Note
that the teacher transcribed the child's explanation of the scene and added his name and
the date.

9

Advantages of Work Samples

• Samples are a valuable resource for teachers as they assess children's progress and share these insights with parents and other teachers
• Work samples may be part of the child's daily activities
• Samples may specifically relate to current instructional objectives
• Collections of work samples enable teachers to quickly locate evidence to support their judgments about children's development

Disadvantages of work samples

• Collection of work samples can be time-consuming, particularly for teachers of large classes
• Teachers need training and practice to understand what to look for in children's work, how to summarize children's progress and how to use the information
• The purpose of tracking children's progress must be clear so that the child's early work is not judged inappropriately
• Collections of work samples can be overwhelming if they are not made selectively

Source: Northwest Regional Educational Laboratory, 1991

Meisels and Steele (1991) suggest that approximately once every two weeks, but no less frequently than monthly, teachers should invite individual children, or small groups of children, to examine their work samples and choose items to be saved in their portfolios. Teachers can guide children in this process, perhaps by saying, "Choose something that was the most difficult for you to do," or "Choose something that you would like to work on again." These suggestions should be noted on the selected items so that those reviewing the portfolio will know how *the child* regarded those pieces of work. It also is very important to note the date of each piece of work as it is filed in the portfolio.

If the teacher wishes to add a work specimen to a child's portfolio, in order to demonstrate a particular skill or developmental characteristic, but the child insists upon taking the work home, the teacher can make a photocopy of the work and give the original to the child. After taking photographs of special events, teachers can have duplicate prints made so that children can keep copies of those, too.

When collected over time, samples of children's work will provide the teacher with visible, concrete clues about the children's fine motor control, perception, attention span and ability to complete tasks (Morrison, 1988). The collection of performance or work samples allows the teacher to gather multiple examples of supporting information about the child's progress in a particular area of development. A primary responsibility of the teacher is to accurately measure the child's success at meeting the objectives of the program. Thus, work samples preserved in a portfolio should reflect the breadth of the program's curriculum and goals. Therefore, information about the goals and curriculum of the overall program, as well as particular goals for individual children, also should be included in portfolios.

Systematic Observations

One of the most common and important assessment techniques that teachers use to gain information about children is *systematic observation*. Observation involves deliberate and thoughtful listening to and watching children's behaviors. The teacher must have clear objectives in mind before observing children so that he can focus on a particular behavior or developmental area. For example, the teacher who decides to observe and record a child's progress in playing cooperatively probably will not record that child's skill at stacking blocks at the same time.

Young children should be observed when they are playing alone, in small groups, and in large groups and at various times of the day and in various circumstances. Effective classroom observation must be systematic, objective, selective, unobtrusive and carefully recorded (Bertrand & Cebula, 1980). The following guidelines can help teachers become systematic observers.

1. Observe exactly what the child does. Record precisely any special, detailed observations of what the child says and does. Note the date, time, setting, what prompted the behavior, and what followed the

behavior. Write down what is actually seen and heard — not opinions or conclusions about the actions.

2. Record observation as soon as possible. Many teachers have developed the skill of facilitating classroom activities and observing children's behavior simultaneously. Observation is a learned skill, however, and will take practice. Plan schedules so that recording information can be done as quickly as possible without disturbing the flow of classroom activities. Details are important but are quickly forgotten if not written down.

3. Observe children within a variety of settings and at different times in the school day. Changes in time and setting will often provide clues about children's moods, interests, styles and patterns of behavior. For example, discovering when and why a child is especially irritable may help in planning changes to insure a smoother day for the child.

4. Be realistic in scheduling observations. If the purpose of the observation is to determine the developmental level of the child, it is critical to observe and make notes as often and in as many situations as necessary to get a complete record of the child's behavior. If observation time is planned, be certain to make the observations.

Advantages of Observational Methods

• The child does not have to read, write or compute in order to be assessed
• Observations can relate to specific current instructional objectives
• Ongoing observation helps detect problems as they arise instead of waiting until the next scheduled assessment
• Observation provides a context that can reveal behavior patterns and changes in patterns

Disadvantages of Observational Methods

• Observations are time-consuming to collect and summarize
• Training and practice often are necessary in order to know what to look for, how to record and how to use information
• Teachers must be free to observe
• Information gathered may be useless unless it is selective and carefully summarized

Source: Northwest Regional Educational Laboratory, 1991

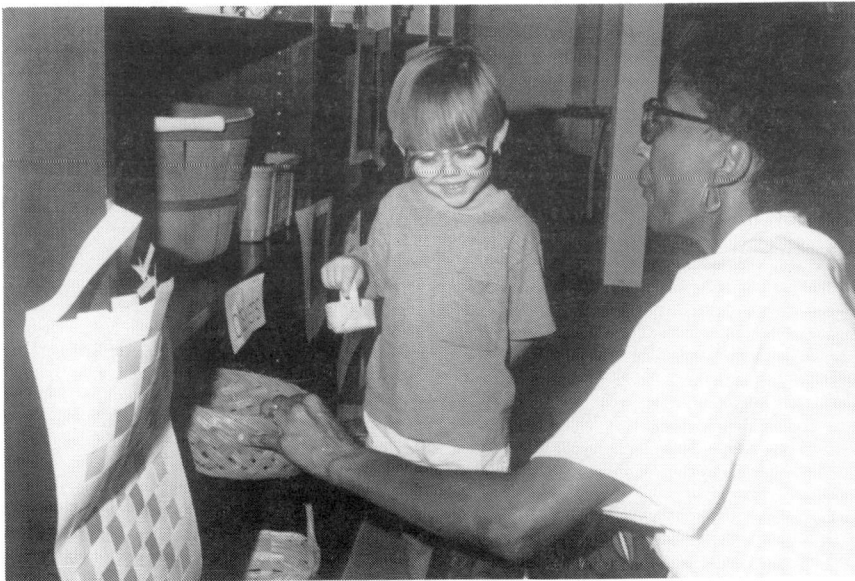

Here a teacher discreetly assesses a child's ability to discriminate between sizes of baskets and to express the relational concept of size. She will record his responses on a checklist or systematic record form.

11

5. Focus on one child at a time. Paying attention to individual children in addition to using checklists or rating scales will help you develop observation skills.

6. Avoid being obvious. Do not call attention to the process of observation or the child being observed. Try to watch the child without disturbing normal interactions or planned activities.

7. Protect confidentiality. Never leave notes where they can be read by other teachers or parents of other children. Never discuss observations in front of other children or parents of other children. A system of coding names may be necessary to protect confidentiality.

8. Choose a workable recording system. Teachers should refer to program goals and objectives as well as individual children's goals when recording information. An example of a systematic record form appears in Appendix C. One may need to experiment with file cards, notebooks, and three-ring binders to determine exactly what process works best . The purpose and method of observation would help determine the system (Cook, Tessier, & Armbruster, 1987).

Anecdotal Records

Anecdotal records are factual, nonjudgmental observations of observed activity (Northwest Regional Educational Laboratory, 1991). They are most useful for recording unanticipated events. Direct quotes and descriptions of children's gestures and expressions are especially valuable in these records. The format in the example that begins on this page is a convenient device for recording these events quickly. A sample format is provided in Appendix D. While anecdotal records are brief, describing only one incident at a time, they are cumulative and can provide a detailed picture of the child if reviewed in a sequential manner. Teachers' notes to themselves about why they recorded these events will add perspective to the record later. However, it is important for the teacher to separate her observation from her intention in recording the observation (Beaty, 1990).

Teachers should not draw conclusions about children's behavioral patterns from one or two anecdotal reports, but rather from a series of observations recorded over time. These guidelines help teachers develop good anecdotal records.

1. Determine what to observe. Choose which behaviors are important to monitor. Teachers should record behaviors that relate to program goals as well as objectives for individual children.

2. Keep the anecdote in context. Recording a particular action in isolation will not yield much information. Date, time, classroom setting, and

Tom: Four years, eight months

Date: Sept. 28
Observation: Tom wrote his name and the words cat, mama, Sam and car, using well-formed letters. He uses many colors when he draws at the art table. Today he drew a picture. It contained recognizable animals, a mermaid and a unicorn. Tom told me a very long story about his drawing. He used long sentences with many descriptor words. In drawing his picture, Tom wanted to use a blue crayon that Mary was using. He tried to grab the crayon from her. She refused to let go of it. Tom threw the remainder of the crayons on the floor and put his head down at the center for 3-4 minutes. He then proceeded with his drawing, picking up crayons as he needed them.
Comments: Tom is especially creative at the art table. He seems to work well with others as long as things go his

other factual information should be noted.

3. Make the anecdote specific. The more precisely and simply a teacher reports behavior, the easier it will be to analyze. General and rambling narratives about behavior can cloud the real issue that needs to be examined.

4. Keep the anecdote objective. A good rule of thumb is that if the teacher wishes to express his reaction to an incident or make an evaluative comment, he should note those in parentheses and keep them separate from the actual report of the incident.

5. Keep the recording process simple. Anecdotal records should not become a chore or take too much time from teaching and learning. However, adequate information should be collected to make a sound judgment.

These records can be reviewed periodically with other information in the portfolio to better understand a child's growth and development.

The Checklist or Inventory

The checklist or inventory is one of the easiest tools for recording children's progress. It should be based upon instructional objectives, and the developmental pattern associated with acquisition of the skills being monitored, with different items clearly defined. By analyzing checklists, teachers can verify their observations without having to rely on memory. The checklist also helps the teacher plan instruction to meet the needs of individual children.

Checklists can be developed to monitor any behavior. They are often divided into sections for each area of development, including intellectual, social, emotional and physical growth. Checklists are appropriate for use when the behaviors to be observed can be anticipated and when there is no need to record the quality or quantity of the performance (Northwest Regional Educational Laboratory, 1991). Appendix A contains the Kindergarten Checklist developed by the Hattiesburg, Mississippi Public Schools. The checklist is divided into four categories: (1) Social and Emotional, (2) Verbal, Cognitive and Linguistic, (3) Visual Perception, and (4) Pre-number and Number Concepts. Each category contains several subcategories and a section for recording the child's growth over time.

In general, observations should be based on regular activities, not on specially-constructed or artificial activities. Sometimes checklist items may require teachers to set up specific situations to enable children to demonstrate their abilities. Schickendanz et al. (1990) call the use of classroom activities to gather information "contrived information gathering". The word "contrived" is used to show that an activity is specifically planned to help the teacher assess the child. For example, waiting for a chance to observe whether Sally can hop on one foot

way. He cries or pouts easily when he has to compromise with another child or change his plan.

Date: Oct. 29, morning
Observation: I asked Tom to put his blocks away to get ready for snack. He said, "I hate snack" and crossed his arms and looked out the window. I explained he could return to the center later. He ignored me but in 3-4 minutes picked up the blocks and came to snack with a smile.

Date: Oct. 29, afternoon
Observation: I asked the children to leave their work centers so we could go outside. Tom remained after the others were lined up. I went to him and again told him he could return to the center after outside time. He responded, "I hate going outside."
Comments: It seems that Tom has difficulty moving from one activity to another. He also seems to quickly recover from his anxiety about change, especially if I reassure him.

Date: Nov. 20
Observation: Tom identified the letters A-Z today while playing an alphabet lotto game. He identified the letters out of sequence.

Date: Nov. 22
Observation: During our large motor activity, Tom turned a cartwheel, skipped and danced in time to the music. He pushed Tony when Tony wouldn't get out of "his space". When Tony told Tom to stop, Tom began to cry and kicked a nearby chair.
Comments: Tom still pouts or gets angry easily when things don't go his way. Sometimes I can talk to him and it subsides, sometimes I ignore it and it

goes away quickly. He is always interested in group time and the stories I read to the group.

Date: Feb. 13

Observation: Tom would not allow Mary Ann to look at a book he had placed in a pile for when he "got time to look at it". When I told him to give her the book he threw it at her. Tom beat his fist on the floor and yelled "No, no, no!" for 1-2 minutes. I placed him in time out until he gained control enough for us to talk about the problem. He said he was sorry. "I like you and Mary Ann, please don't be mad." He told me his mom was getting married this weekend and that he had a new Dad and brother. He said he would try harder to be "nice."

Comments: I am talking with Tom about how to deal with anger and how to let someone know you are mad in a away that is acceptable. We are going to work on alternatives to kicking, screaming and throwing objects. I am going to promote that he talk his "mad" out. His vocabulary is large enough that he can do it if he realizes that is his first way to respond. (His mother's marriage and change in his family life may be a reason that changes in the classroom are hard for him right now. I intend to watch him closely at transition times.)

Source: Teri Patrick, University of Arkansas at Little Rock Children's Center. Unpublished anecdotal record. (The child's name has been changed.)

might take a long time. Months might pass before Sally is in a situation that calls for hopping on one foot — and when it occurs, the teacher might be looking the other way.

A variety of activities that are found in learning centers or provided during teacher-initiated group activities can be used as vehicles for observing children's skills and accomplishments. Singing, fingerplays, games, and problem-solving activities are opportunities for the child to demonstrate progress while participating in real classroom activities. Songs and fingerplays are particularly good activities for teachers to observe because they reveal so much about what children know and are capable of doing. For example, "Five Elephants Went Out to Play" will reveal which children can say numerals in sequence. (However, a word of caution is needed. Teachers must be aware that children may be able to sing a song that names the numerals up to ten and yet be unable to count ten objects. To judge whether a child can *count*, they must be given a genuine counting task involving one-to-one correspondence.)

Songs and fingerplays also can be used to gather information about chil-

Here a teacher assesses a child's ability to count the animals in an illustration in a magazine which he has chosen. She unobtrusively notes on a checklist how high he can count.

14

dren's physical skills and knowledge as well as their interests and areas of talent, creativity and social skills. "Head, Shoulders, Knees and Toes" can be used both to teach the parts of the body and to measure a child's motor ability, coordination and knowledge of body parts. Asking children to make up a song, dance or rap can give the teacher information about their abilities in music, bodily-kinesthetic and poetry.

Many of the games regularly played in classrooms can be used for informal assessment. Knowledge of such concepts as numbers, shapes and animals can be measured as well as knowledge of children's social skills. Lotto-style or bingo-style games are excellent because they are available commercially or easily made to relate to almost any topic. Other information can be gathered by watching *how* the children play games. Who can follow directions? Who lacks confidence and wants to check his work by comparing it to other children's work? Who persists at challenging tasks? Games which involve spinners or die add other dimensions to the teacher's unobtrusive assessment. Since so much information can be discerned, teachers should decide which specific behaviors to observe *before* initiating such activities.

By observing children at learning centers as they play with other children and interact with materials, the teacher has other opportunities to unobtrusively record children's achievements and interests. Through this technique, the child may be viewed in a variety of situations and engaged in a variety of activities. Teale (1990) recommends that dramatic play areas be modified to reveal information about children's knowledge of print and literacy. For example, creating a mock post office in a kindergarten classroom allows children to experiment with letters and the use of symbols. It also enables the teacher to observe the children's ability to make sense of those letters and symbols. As another example, the art center can be used by the teacher to measure a child's progress in combining materials, shapes and colors to make collages and other two-dimensional projects.

Special classroom activities and projects can be valuable tools for teachers as they promote problem-solving skills among the children they teach. For example, by making graham cracker treats, children learn the origin of certain foods, how substances can change if exposed to a changing environment (sudden heat or cold), and how to cooperate with others in completing a task. By asking questions such as "How can we make graham cracker treats?" and "What things do we need?", teachers invite children to demonstrate knowledge and skills. If they provide a variety of toppings and instruct children to make their own treats, teachers can observe the children synthesize or think creatively.

Rating Scales

Rating scales are appropriately used when the behavior to be observed has several different aspects or components (Northwest Regional Educational Laboratory, 1991). Each behavior is rated on a continuum that goes from the lowest to the highest level and is marked off at certain points along the scale. The observer must judge where a child's behavior lies on the scale (Beaty, 1990). An example of a graphic scale appears on this page. This rating scale measures only one behavior, making it easier to construct than to use. The teacher must know the child well, be able to interpret his behavior and be able to make an objective judgment in a short time.

Rating scales also may be in numerical form. The teacher observes a child as long as it takes to check a number for each skill or behavior to be measured, or

CHILD'S NAME

Nikki Washington

BEHAVIOR

Shares toys

FREQUENCY (circle one)

Daily
Several times a week
Once a week
Bimonthly
Never

An example of a graphic scale.

Sam Little

CHILD'S NAME

KEY

1 = needs more time or assistance
2 = satisfactory
3 = excellent

BEHAVIORS	DATE	RATING
Follows single one-step directions		
Follows multi-step directions		
Attends to teacher-directed small group discussions, story telling or reading		
Reproduces rhythmic pattern (clap/snap)		

An example of a numerical scale.

the teacher observes the child daily and then averages those scores (Beaty, 1990).

Interviews

One of the most effective and easy means of gathering information is to ask the child direct questions. Handing a child an object and asking him to tell you about it can be very effective in determining whether he recognizes the object and understands its uses and social significance. Open-ended requests such as "I'd like you to tell me about this" elicit samples of the child's expressive language ability.

Asking children about their behavior often yields insights into why they behave as they do. One teacher of five-year-olds encourages her children to talk about their problems even though she knows that they cannot always describe exactly what worries them. She explains, "Even though they can't always tell me what the problem is in words, many times I can tell whether it is a school problem, a home problem, or a problem with another child. This gives me the clue I need to begin to find a solution."

Teachers can ask parents about events prior to children's joining the class in order to acquire background information that may relate to children's current

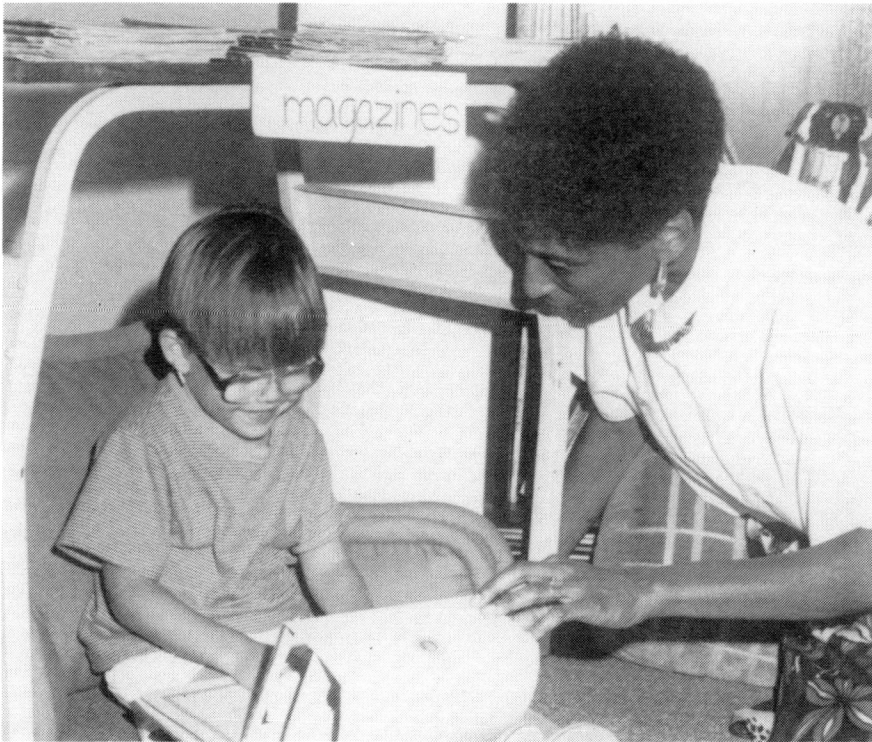

By asking the child, "Tell me why you like this pop-up book," the teacher invites him to demonstrate expressive language ability without creating a stressful testing situation.

17

behavior. One teacher of three- and four-year-olds was experiencing a great deal of trouble in helping a new student, Tom, adjust to the class rest time. He grew more agitated each day for a week. By the fifth day, his temper tantrums and refusal to lie on his mat prompted the teacher to have a conference with Tom's mother. By interviewing his mother, the teacher learned that Tom's older brother had teased Tom about his new school and told him that if he ever went to sleep at school he would miss the bus and be left behind. Although Tom's mother had dismissed the remark as "kids' talk", Tom obviously had not. Once the teacher and parent both understood the situation, they were able to help Tom overcome his fear.

Through interviews with parents, teachers can learn much about children's behavior at home and how it affects their experiences at school. This helps teachers understand how children transfer the concepts, skills and information acquired in the classroom to life outside the classroom. Parents may also provide their perspective of the social and emotional climate in the home. The type and amount of information gathered through interviews with parents depends heavily upon the interviewing skills of the teacher.

Screening Tests and Developmental Scales

Screening tests are used to help identify the skills and strengths that children already possess so that teachers can plan meaningful learning experiences for their pupils. For example, a teacher may alter her curriculum plan after discovering through the use of a developmental scale that most children in her class have already acquired a particular concept.

The assessment information revealed by such instruments is *not* appropriately used for grading, labeling, grouping or retaining children. Rather, findings of screening tests and developmental scales should be considered along with work samples and other more subjective material which the teacher assembles in the portfolio.

The Northwest Regional Educational Laboratory has evaluated several widely-used tests and reported its findings in the table found in Appendix E. It is important to note the definitions and explanations that appear in the key to fully understand those findings.

In choosing an instrument, teachers should consider carefully their program goals, the individual children's needs and the purpose for using a test or scale. Teachers must understand the items used in a test or scale for screening and what the results indicate before they can explain them adequately to parents. At any time they feel uncertain about the screening instrument or scores, teachers should consult a testing specialist. *SACUS does not recommend routine, mass use of standardized tests or scales.*

This chapter has focused on the major components of the assessment portfolio. The information about children's achievements and development which is contained in portfolios should help teachers make comprehensive decisions about program curriculum, instructional methods and, of course, the progress of individual children.

18

References

Beaty, J. (1990). *Observing development of the young child* (2nd ed.). Columbus, OH: Merrill Publishing Co.

Bertrand, A. & Cebula, J. (1980). *Tests, measurement, and evaluation: A developmental approach.* Reading, MA: Adison-Wesley.

Carini, P. (1978). Documentary processes. Paper presented at the annual meeting of the American Research Association, Toronto.

Cook, R.E.; Tessler, A., & Armbruster, V.B. (1987). *Adapting early childhood curricula for children with special needs.* Columbus, OH: Charles E. Merrill.

Engel, B. (1990). An approach to assessment in early literacy. In C. Kamii (Ed.), *Achievement testing in the early grades: The games grown-ups play.* Washington, D.C.: National Association for the Education of Young Children.

Faddis, B. (1991). Alternative program evaluation ideas for early childhood education programs. Portland, OR: Northwest Regional Educational Laboratory.

Hattiesburg Public Schools. (1988). Kindergarten Checklist. Hattiesburg, MS: Author.

Meisels, S. and Steele, D. (1991). The early childhood portfolio collection process. Center for Human Growth and Development. Ann Arbor, MI: University of Michigan.

Morrison, G. S. (1988). *Early childhood education today* (4th ed.). Columbus, OH: Merrill Publishing Co.

National Association for the Education of Young Children. (1988). Position statement on standardized testing of young children 3 through 8 years of age. Washington, D.C.: Author.

Paulson, F. L., Paulson, P.R. & Meyer, C.A. (1991). What makes a portfolio a portfolio? *Educational Leadership, 48,* 60-63.

Northwest Regional Educational Laboratory. (1991). Alternative program evaluation ideas for early childhood education programs. Portland, OR: Author.

National Association for the Education of Young Children and National Association of Early Childhood Specialists in State Departments of Education. (1991). Guidelines for appropriate curriculum content and assessment in programs serving children age 3 through 8. Washington, D.C.: NAEYC. (NAEYC #725).

Schickendanz, J. A., York, M.E., Stewart, I.S. & White D.A. (1990). *Strategies for teaching young children,* third ed. Englewood Cliffs, N.J.: Prentice-Hall.

Southern Association on Children Under Six. (1990). Developmentally appropriate assessment. Little Rock, AR: Author.

Teale, W.H. (1988). Developmentally appropriate assessment of reading and writing in the early childhood classroom. *Elementary School Journal, 89,* 173-183.

Wortham, S.C. (1984). *Organizing instruction in early childhood: A handbook of assessment and activities.* New York: Allyn and Bacon.

Chapter 3

Using the Assessment Portfolio In Evaluation

Once the child, teacher and parent have gathered material and information for an assessment portfolio, the most important step in the evaluation of the child's development can occur. That step is the *analysis and interpretation* of the portfolio's contents. It is the analysis of the data and the many educational decisions that flow from that analysis that will affect the child. Review and analysis of assessment portolios also enable teachers to revise curriculum and instruction as necessary, so that the process eventually benefits every child in the program.

Organizing the Portfolio

The material in a portfolio should be organized by category and in time sequence for ease of reference. Since all information in the portfolio is dated, sequencing the work samples, interviews, checklists, inventories, screening test results or other information should be simple. Some teachers find it helpful to organize the portfolio in an expandable folder using dividers so that the child's work can be easily filed and selected. For larger samples of artwork, x-ray folders or carefully cleaned pizza boxes are adequate. Date stamps are a quick way for the teacher (or child!) to note when the work was done. Blank gummed labels or self-sticking removable notes are useful for attaching observations and comments. It should be noted that some work cannot be easily classified. Much can be learned from observing how children define, evaluate and classify their own work.

The following outline suggests how to organize a portfolio for preschool and primary grade children (Meisels and Steele, 1991).

Art Activities (Fine Motor Development)
> •Drawings of events, persons, and animals. The child might dictate descriptions or explanations of the drawings to the teacher or a parent or classroom volunteer. Or the child might write such explanations. (The teacher may need to make notes if the child writes his own picture caption.)
> • Photos of unusual block constructions or projects, labeled and dated.
> • Collages and other examples of the child's use of various media when designing a picture.
> •Samples of the child's manuscript printing. (The appearance and placement of the letters on the page are evaluated in the context of a developmental continuum.)

"Unlike standardized assessments that are little more than a "snapshot" of a child's performance on a single occasion, portfolios capture the evolution of a child's abilities, providing a rich documentation of each child's experience throughout the year."

Samuel J. Meisels and Dorothy M. Steele, 1991

The teacher should always note the child's name and the date on a work sample before placing it in the child's portfolio. Here a teacher uses a cardboard pizza box to contain a portfolio.

Movement (Gross Motor Development)
> •Notes recorded by the teacher or video tapes of the child's movement activities in the classroom or on the playground, which reflect the child's developing skills.
> •Notes, photographs, video tapes and anecdotal records which demonstrate the child's skills and progress in music activities and fingerplays
> •Notes from teacher interviews with the child about his favorite active games at school

Math and Science Activities (Concept Development)
> •Photographs of the child measuring or counting specific ingredients as part of a cooking activity
> •Charts on which the child has recorded the planting, care, watering schedule, periods of sunlight, etc., of plants in the classroom or on the school grounds.
> •Work samples demonstrating the child's understanding of number concepts. An example is the numeral four formed with beans glued to a sheet of paper and the appropriate number of beans glued beside the numeral.
> •Work samples, teacher notes, taped pupil interviews illustrating, in a

22

progressive fashion, the child's understanding of mathematical concepts. (Examples are counting sets of objects, combining those sets and then recounting the new set. This activity demonstrates the child's understanding of the concept of addition, given that the child was able to verbalize her actions while engaged in the task.)

•Photographs and data gathered from checklists and taped pupil interviews which document the child's conceptual understanding, exploring, hypothesizing and problem-solving. (The documentation will depend upon the child's developmental stages during the life of the portfolio.) A checklist the child completes, in which she guesses which object will float prior to putting the objects in the water, and then notes which items actually do float, is an example of data that demonstrates the child's conceptual understanding, hypothesizing, and observational skill.

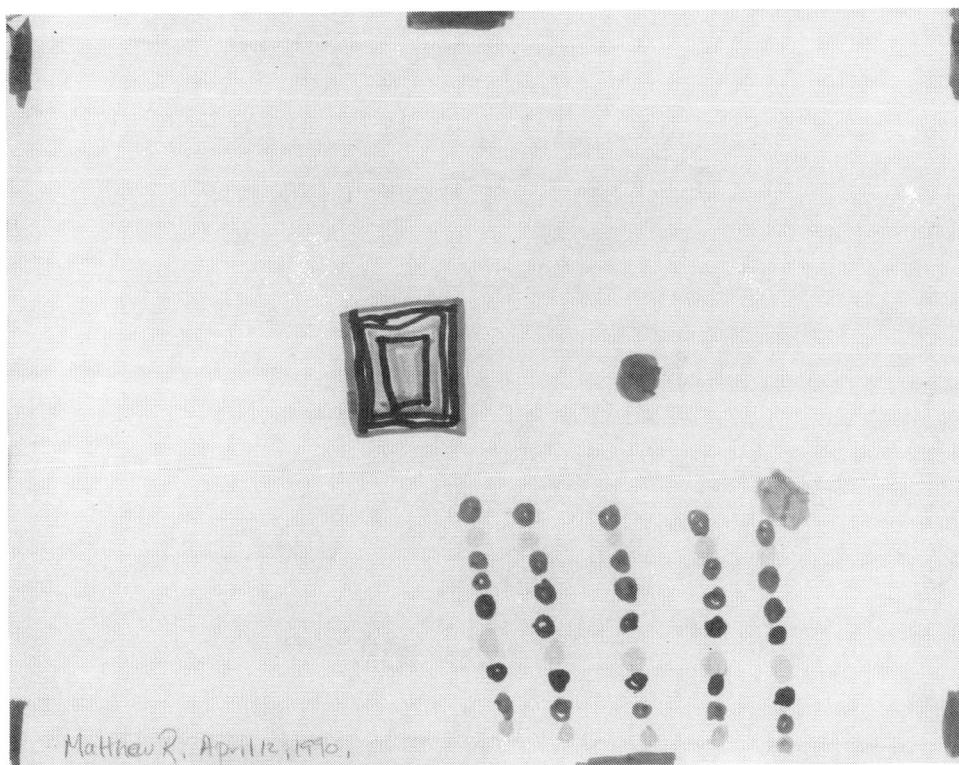

Matthew R, April 12, 1990.

This work sample indicates that the child understands patterning, an essential mathematics concept. Pink, blue, green, light and dark purple, yellow, red, pink and green are used in identical order in each series of carefully formed circles. Note the careful orange markings in the corners and top and bottom centers of the paper. They indicate that the child is in the early schematic stage in drawing. (See the section, "Assessing Fine Motor Development and Concept Development.")

23

Language and Literacy

•Tape recordings of a child re-reading stories which she "wrote" or dictated to a parent, teacher or classroom volunteer.

•Examples of the child's journal entries.

•Copies of signs or labels the child contructed.

• A log of book titles actually read by the child or read to the child by a teacher, parent or other adult.

•Copies of stories, poems, or songs the child wrote or dictated.

•Taped pupil interviews that reveal the child's increase, over time, in vocabulary and skill in use of the language.

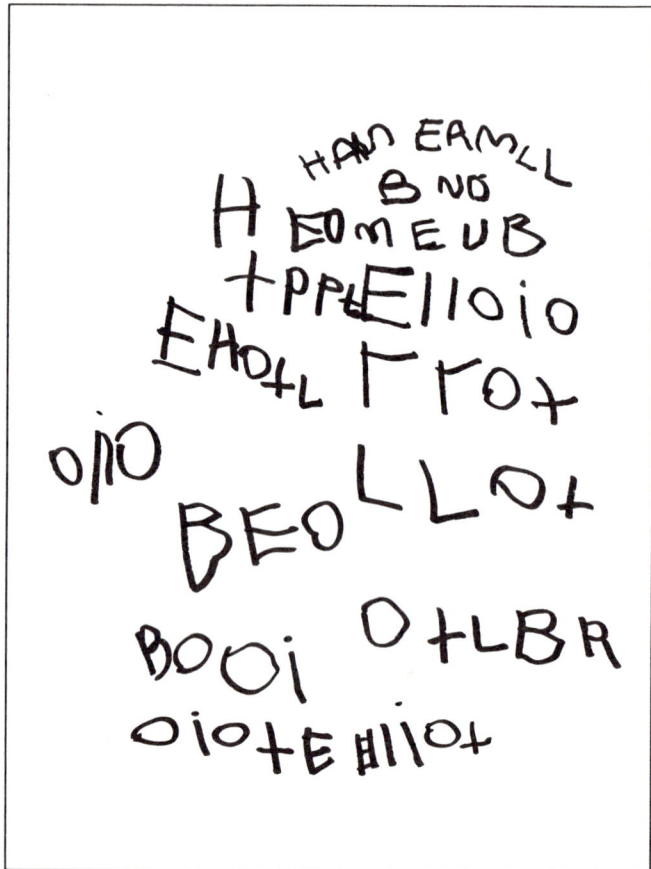

The work that children produce of their own initiative is a better indication of their development than the score on a standardized test. Here a child's writing is clear evidence of his emerging literacy. The child has written from top to bottom and from left to right. He is able to form recognizable letters. If the teacher had been present when he wrote this piece, she could have asked him to "read" it to her and then transcribed his dictation, thus preserving the intent of his invented spelling.

Personal and Social Development

•Teacher notes and anecdotal records that document interactions between the child and her peers. Such interactions can indicate the child's ability to make choices, solve problems, and cooperate with others.

•Teacher notes, anecdotal records, and video-recordings that document events that occured on field trips. Such incidents may illustrate the child's social awareness.

•Chart of the child's choices of activities during a particular week or month. (A sample chart appears in Appendix B.)

•Notes from teacher-parent conferences.

Evaluating Children and Evaluating Curriculum

Once the portfolio is organized, the teacher can evaluate the child's achievements. Appropriate evaluation always compares the child's current work to the *same child's earlier work*. It does not compare the child's work to that of other children. This evaluation should indicate the child's progress toward a standard of performance. That standard must be *consistent with the teacher's curriculum* and with *appropriate developmental expectations*. This means, for example, that a teacher of five-year-olds does not conclude that a child is slow to develop because he is unable to spell correctly and write legibly his first and last names, for that particular goal is not reasonable for five-year-olds and therefore is not developmentally appropriate in a program for five-year-olds. On the other hand, a five-year-old's ability to write his first and last names is noteworthy in a portfolio, because it indicates an unusual understanding of symbols and well-developed fine motor skills.

It is clear, then, that the teacher's standards of progress are critical to the value and effectiveness of an assessment portfolio. If a program includes developmentally appropriate goals, all children will, *over time*, show progress toward those standards (Meisels and Steele, 1991). We emphasize the child's progress over time to stress that a portfolio must be longitudinal. A collection of work samples gathered over a few weeks will reveal little about a child's development. To be meaningful, the samples must be preserved in the portfolio over the entire period that the child is enrolled in the program.

Placing a copy of the program objectives or standards of progress in each child's portfolio therefore is helpful to the teacher as well as the parent. As the teacher reviews the material, he will have the context of his program goals immediately at hand. During conferences with parents, the copy of program goals is useful again in explaining the child's various activities.

By regularly checking the materials in the portfolio, the teacher can note that the child's progress in one area is not being adequately documented. The balance should not be restored with hurried, unnatural activities created to "fill in the gap", but rather with the teacher's reasonable observations. Should it appear that *all of the children* in the class are underrepresented in a particular area, the teacher will need to reexamine the curriculum and daily schedule to determine if she is adequately addressing the area in question. For example, a lack of

25

anecdotes about interaction on the playground might indicate a lack of outside free play in the schedule.

The same is true when a teacher reviews a portfolio and notices an overabundance of samples from a particular curricular area, such as journal entries. Is it indicative of too much emphasis on journal-writing, to the point of excluding other equally important curriculum or developmental areas? In this way, evaluation of the portfolio helps the teacher evaluate the program curriculum and modify it as necessary.

In reviewing data in a child's portfolio, the teacher should pay careful attention to the areas which require reteaching. Using the information obtained from teacher observations based on checklists, inventories or rating scales will assist the teacher in planning for and meeting individual needs. Gathering initial information about a child before teaching particular concepts or skills enables the teacher to wisely use instructional time and create an inviting and challenging learning environment for the child.

Portfolios are not meant to be used for comparing one child to another. They are used to document individuals' progress over time. It should go without saying that the material assembled in the portfolio must accurately represent the child's work and progress and justify the teacher's assessments. If a parent, administrator, other teacher or outside expert examines the portfolio, he should be able to reach similiar conclusions as the teacher about the student's abilities and achievements.

The teacher's conclusions about the child's achievements, abilities, strengths, weaknesses and needs should be based on the full range of the child's development, as documented by the data in the portfolio, and on the teacher's knowledge of curriculum and growth stages in various areas of development. The following two examples show how developmental sequences can be used in evaluating the information found in a portfolio. If should be noted that teachers should use a comprehensive compilation of developmental stages and characteristics when evaluating the entire portfolio.

Assessing Personal and Social Development

A teacher made the following anecdotal record:

> Shauna was observed in the house center. She was carrying an infant doll in the crook of one arm and moving pots and pans back and forth between the table and the stove while talking to herself and the doll. "You be a good girl or mommy will spank you. Eat all your peas, that's a good girl." Other children in the center are stacking clothes and making the bed.

To evaluate that episode, the teacher would have to consider the six stages of social play, as described by Mildred Parton in 1932:

1. Unoccupied play. Children wander and watch.

26

2. Onlooker. Children watch others play, ask questions and make suggestions but do not participate.

3. Solitary play. Children select toys with which to play but are not interested in other children's activities.

4. Parallel play. The child plays near another child and may play with the same objects, but does not interact.

5. Associative play. Children play with others, are engaged in activities, and may exclude some children, but rarely negotiate about the direction their play takes.

6. Cooperative play. Children organize their play, assigning roles and negotiating turns.

According to Parton, the teacher could characterize the episode at the house center as a *parallel social play experience* since Shauna played in the same area and near other children, but did not interact with them. Observing Shauna throughout the year, using Parton's stages of social play as a guide, the teacher can document Shauna's development in the area of social play.

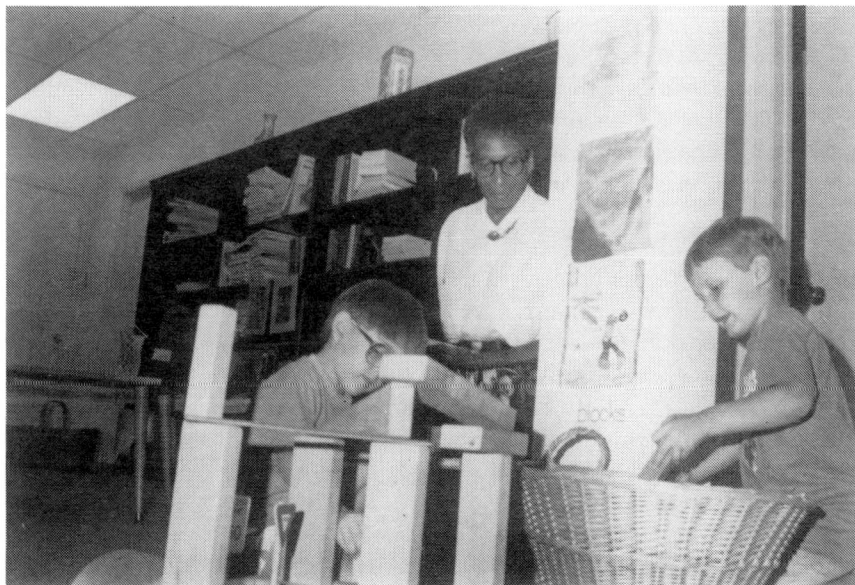

Teachers must understand the normal stages of personal and social development before they can competently assess and evaluate young children. Here a teacher observes the interaction of two children at play with blocks. She gathers rich information about the boys' social development without the children being aware of the assessment process.

In evaluating children's artwork, the teacher evaluates the child's progress over time. In other words, What developmental stage does a drawing represent? And, does the drawing indicate progress *when compared to earlier work*?

Children's artwork can be in various media, including paper, paint, modeling clay and "found objects" such as cast-off boxes. In each medium, a child typically passes through several stages. These stages of development of children ages two to nine years have been delineated by numerous experts (Lowenfeld, 1954; Kellogg, 1970; Lowenfeld & Brittain, 1987). The examples on the following pages demonstrate the basic stages.

The first stage is usually called the *scribble or exploration stage,* during which the child discovers what the medium can do and what can be done to the medium. These scribbles are basically uncontrolled and unnamed by the child. Children at this stage often paint many colors over each other as they discover their power to change what they are creating. They shape, squash and reshape clay. Cutting paper is a satisfying experience in itself.

The child labels or gives names to some or all of her work in the *controlled scribble stage.* If she has already experimented with art media, this usually occurs around the age of three years. The child may draw more apparent forms and may elaborate on a shape by painting colors within it or placing dots around the shape (Bland, 1957). Their pictures may contain several renditions of a particular shape, or just one elaborate one. They often cover the entire piece of paper as they draw. In clay, these children are more deliberate and, again, create objects to which they give names.

During a child's *preschematic stage,* teachers can identify designs and representations. Clay forms become more complete and combine shapes. Children use scissors with more skills, cutting actual shapes from paper.

As children enter the *schematic stage,* sky lines (usually blue) and base lines (usually green) appear on the top and bottom of their drawings. Items drawn between these lines usually are somewhat proportionate and are on the baseline when appropriate. This typically occurs between the ages of six and nine years.

It is critical for teachers and parents to understand that, since all children go through the same stages of development, but at different times, *children in a particular classroom or of a particular age are not likely to be in the same developmental stages.* The examples of artwork which appear on the following pages illustrate that, over time, a portfolio can document the individual's progression through the various stages.

Portfolio data collection helps the teacher come to know the child in depth. In the process of that aquaintance the teacher may sense that normal developmental progression is being disrupted or thwarted. When a teacher feels that a child in her class is in need of more specialized evaluation, it is her professional obligation to consult the parents and, with their permission, then consult specialists in the area of concern. The teacher's awareness and use of such material is the critical factor in the success of the portfolio as an evaluation tool.

Marc Renglii   12-7-90

An example of the scribble stage. This child was experimenting with the different markers' colors and with the results of using one color over another.

An example of the controlled scribble stage.

An example of the preschematic stage

An example of the schematic stage

References

Bland, J.C. (1957) *Art of the young child*. New York: Simon and Schuster.

Correro, G. (1988). "Understanding assessment in young children". *Developing Instructional Programs K-3*. Jackson, MS: Mississippi Department of Education, Author.

Howard, E. (1987). Recording data in the classroom. Unpublished work. Starkville, MS: Mississippi State University

Kellogg, R. (1970). *Analyzing children's art*. Palo Alto, CA: Mayfield.

Lowenfeld, V. and Brittain, W.L. (1987). *Creative and mental growth*, 8th ed. New York: Macmillan.

Lowenfeld, V. (1954). *Your child and his art*. New York: MacMillan.

Meisels, S. and Steele, D. (1991). *The early childhood portfolio collection process*. Center for Human Growth and Development. Ann Arbor, MI: University of Michigan.

Parton, M. (1932) "Social participation among pre-school children," *Journal of Abnormal and Social Psychology*, 27:3. pp 243-269.

Resources

Beaty, J. (1990). *Observing developing of the young child* (2nd ed.). Columbus, OH: Merrill Publishing Co.

Bentzen, W. R. (1985). *Seeing young children: A guide to observing and recording behavior*. Albany, NY: Delmar Publishers, Inc.

Bredekamp, S. (Ed.). (1987). *Developmentally appropriate practice in early childhood education: Serving children from birth through Age 8*. Washington, D.C.: National Association for the Education of Young Children.

Hendrick, J. (1988). *The whole child; Developmental education for the early years* (4th ed.). Columbus, OH: Merrill Publishing Co.

Morrison, G. (1988). *Early childhood education today* (4th ed.). Columbus, OH: Merrill Publishing Co.

Northeast Foundation for Children. (1987). *A notebook for teachers: Making changes in the elementary curriculum*. New Haven, CT: Author.

Seefeldt, C. and Barbour, N. (1990). *Early childhood education; An introduction* (2nd ed.). Columbus, OH: Merrill Publishing Co.

Chapter 4

Using the Assessment Portfolio to Communicate with Parents

Using portfolios as the means to assess young children provides teachers with a built-in system for planning parent-teacher conferences. The content of the portfolio provides the basis for discussion. Parents may feel intimidated by the idea of a parent-teacher conference, particularly if they have never attended one before or if their only contact with the teacher or school has been unpleasant. The teacher's use of the portfolio should help put the parent at ease due to the fact that both parent and teacher are looking at concrete examples of the child's work and not discussing the child's progress in the abstract.

In preparing for a conference, the teacher should arrange furniture so that parent and teacher are on the same side of the desk or table—reviewing the work as equals, both interested in the progress made by the child. If audio or video tapes are to be used in the conference, the appropriate equipment should be ready and in place before parents arrive.

After arranging the conference area to allow for a comfortable, pleasant conversation, a teacher shows parents the contents of their child's portfolio. A conversation about the child's interests, activities and achievements is far more meaningful and less stressful to most parents than a discussion of test scores.

The teacher should provide background information as to the circumstances of work samples. Dates when work was completed should be noted to the parent and a continuum of samples should be ready for consideration. As they present the samples, teachers should explain relevant developmental characteristics of children. For example, a writing sample that includes many reversed letters might alarm parents of a five-year-old, suggesting to them that their child has a learning problem. The teacher should explain that backward writing is typical of five-year-olds.

Teachers should also review the findings of checklists and inventories, noting the times of the observations and whether they will be repeated during the year. Explanation of screening tests results should be done as thoroughly as possible. When areas of weakness are noted, the teacher should explain how the curriculum or teaching practice has been modified to help address the child's needs.

Teachers should provide written suggestions for parents to implement at home, thoroughly explaining them during the conference. At no time should the parent be made to feel guilty or angry at the child for his performance. Young children's development is often uneven and can advance dramatically over a relatively short period with encouragement and the proper environmental stimulation.

"When will my child learn to read?"

Every preschool and primary grade teacher has had a worried parent ask, "But when will my child learn to read?" Assessment portfolios can be very valuable as teachers answer this question and as they discuss young children's development in general.

To reassure a parent who is concerned that her child is "behind" in the race to learn reading and writing, a teacher can pull out examples of invented spelling; lists of books which the child and a teacher, caregiver or aide have read together, or a collage in which the child incorporated the names of cereals and candy bars which he recognized and cut from magazines. In addition, the teacher can describe the fingerplays that the child enjoys during circle time and the "WATCH OUT!" signs which he erected at a construction project made of blocks. The teacher can explain that these activities and work samples each indicate the child's progressive acquisition of language concepts.

At the same time, the teacher can reassure the worried mother or father that *there is no race.* Given appropriate books, toys, games, and art materials, and the encouragement and support of thoughtful parents and teachers, virtually every child will learn to read, some a little sooner than others, but all of them in plenty of time to succeed in school and in life.

Here are a few other examples of the ways in which portfolios can answer parents' questions:

Even though we bought a large jungle gym, Susan never wants to play outside when she is at home. Do you think she has some difficulty using her arms and legs?

By pulling out the activity chart in Susan's portfolio, the preschool teacher can show her mother or father that Susan does routinely join other children in playground games. One systematic record notes that Susan played adeptly on the school's climbing structure, while a checklist verifies that she is capable of throwing and catching a large ball and of playing hopscotch. Yet anecdotal records reveal that Susan tends to choose more sendentary "pretend" games with a few other girls. By asking the parent questions, the teacher may discover that no other small girls live in Susan's immediate neighborhood and that she has no playmates when she goes outside. Perhaps Susan is reluctant to play alone, rather than feeling hesitant to run, jump or climb.

After learning from a parent that a child usually chooses sendentary activities at home as well as at school, a teacher may make a note to give that child extra encouragement to participate in physical activities, in order to promote adequate exercise.

I've noticed the artwork which you have displayed on the walls. My child's drawings do not seem to be as good as the other children's. Is something wrong?

Sean may in fact be in an earlier developmental stage as far as artwork and fine motor control are concerned -- and the teacher may be happy for an opportunity to discuss this with his mother. Using Sean's own crayon drawings and tempera paintings as illustrations, the teacher can confirm that, "Yes, Sean is not as far along as some of the children in this area." She can explain that all children go through the same stages as they experiment with crayons and paint, and that while Sean is still in the *controlled scribble stage*, several of his classmates are in the *schematic stage*. Pointing out that some of those children are six to nine months older than Sean, or that one little girl's father is an artist and so she has had unusual access to art supplies from a very early age, probably will reassure Sean's mother.

Matthew still sucks his thumb although he is almost six years old. Our dentist says we shouldn't worry about it yet, but we wonder -- does he suck his thumb very much at school?

A teacher who makes regular anecdotal records of her young pupils' behavior probably has developed a keen ability to notice and remember details such as whether Matthew sucks his thumb very much. The teacher might be able to respond immediately, "I have noted in my records that Matthew only sucks his thumb when he holds his security blanket, and that he only takes the blanket from his cubby at naptime or when he has bumped his head or tripped on the playground. It seems to me that he is a happy, secure little boy and that his thumb-sucking is limited and does not indicate any underlying problems."

If she does not find anything in her anecdotal records about Matthew's thumb-sucking, the teacher can promise to keep a systematic record of his thumb-sucking over the next five days and then call the parent with a report.

As you know, we are going to move to another state in a couple of months. We have tried to talk to Melanie about this, but she doesn't seem to listen. Do you have any ideas?

By looking at drawings that Melanie has recently made at the art center, her teacher and parents can discover that she has frequently chosen houses as a subject. In fact, a series of drawings done over several weeks seem to be of the same house -- and her parents confirm that it appears to be their home.

Anecdotal records made by another teacher of Melanie's play at the house-keeping center describe repeated enactments of "moving time". Melanie packed all of the toy pots and pans and doll clothes into a child's suitcase and carried them about, telling the dolls, "It's time to go. Don't worry; you will have a new room with all of your things in it."

Although few classroom teachers have the background or skills necessary to make psychological judgments about their students, it seems clear in this example that Melanie has listened to her parents' reassurances and is coping with the upcoming move her own ways.

Just as every child is unique, the questions and concerns that parents and teachers have about individual children are unique. These hypothetical examples should demonstrate that portfolios can be far more valuable than standardized tests in tracing children's social, academic, physical and emotional development -- and in communicating their progress to parents and future teachers.

Chapter Five

The Assessment Portfolio as an Attitude

The teacher's use of good judgment is a key to effective assessment of young children. Taking time to think about children and their behavior is very important, whether or not a teacher uses an assessment portfolio. It has been estimated that the average first grade teacher makes about one thousand decisions a day and the average preschool teacher makes twice as many (Jackson, 1968; Murray, 1986). There is little time in the teacher's day to think carefully about individual children and their special needs, yet early childhood professionals must incorporate such "thinking time" into their schedules, not just to plan the next day's activities but to reflect upon the events of the current day. A teacher of three-year-olds once said, "I feel like a detective. There is so much to know and three-year-olds can tell me so little. I would have to guess about everything if I didn't have their behavior to give me clues." This is an example of what can be called *the portfolio attitude*.

Teachers begin to assemble an assessment portfolio by *writing down* these clues, along with their observations, thoughts and questions about individual children. As they collect samples of their pupils' work and observation cards about class and small group games and activities, and as they interview the children to gain more information, teachers assess young children in appropriate ways. The assessment process is a vital part of planning, implementing and maintaining developmentally appropriate practice in the classroom.

In the past, a school might have considered a young child "ready to learn" when he made an acceptable score on a standardized test. Today, however, many school and government officials define "readiness" as the student's being prepared to participate successfully in formal schooling. "Readiness" now has multiple dimensions, the most important being that the child has an orientation toward learning and a certain ability to solve problems. Educators no longer consider first grade the child's first learning experience. Rather, they view first grade as a continuation of the learning process that began at birth.

In response to the shift in public policy, teachers are beginning to use instructional practices that reflect what many have known all the time — that children's concepts of reading and counting, their social skills, and their physical and emotional growth occur over time and in predictable developmental stages. Their innovations in early childhood classrooms are another example of *the portfolio attitude*.

Non-graded primary units are being instituted in public schools and multiage grouping has renewed popularity (Charlesworth, 1989). In 1988 the National Association of State Boards of Education released a report, *Right From the Start*, which set forth recommendations for restructuring schooling of four-through eight-year-olds. The report urged that

> Early childhood units be established in elementary schools to provide a new pedagogy for working with children age 4-8 and a focal point for enhanced services to preschool children and their parents.

All of these events signal the admission by those in education and outside the field that children's learning is a continuous process. Thus, the collection and maintenance of information about the child's learning also should be continuous.

For teachers who always have based instruction and curriculum on their observations of their students, the "fuss about assessment" is bewildering.

For those teachers who have always based the majority of their instructional strategies and curriculum plans on the results of standardized achievement tests, criterion referenced tests based on state-mandated curriculum objectives, or student placement tests such as readiness tests, the "fuss" is intimidating. Some of these teachers are suspicious. Others expect that "this too will pass".

For teachers who are new to the field, the debates over testing, placement and other related issues are confusing and frightening. They may wonder, Who is right? What is right? How do I know if what I choose to do will be the best course of action for the children in my room?

To address the concerns and reactions of these teachers, we should reflect on the old saying that "The more things change, the more they stay the same". In the early history of preschool and primary education, teachers accumulated student work and used it in planning and instruction. Moreover, parents and communities respected the informed judgments of teachers.

Since then, our society has reacted and overreacted to world and national events -- Sputnik, *Why Johnny Can't Read* (Flesch, 1955), integration of public schools, shifts in demographics and in family dynamics. Our educational system has felt the turmoil. By the 1970s and 1980s, *what* was taught, *how* it was taught and *when* it would be taught were largely controlled by curriculum guides, standardized tests and state and federal legislation about school assignments and equal educational opportunities. Teachers, once valued as the experts on children's development, seemed to gradually lose the public's respect and, with that, the authority to plan how to meet their students' needs.

With government guarantees of equal educational opportunity has come ever-greater government bureacracy -- until many teachers' feel their spirits have been broken and the sense of community within many schools and school districts has diminished.

Standardized testing is one dimensional and only depicts the child's brief engagement with an unnatural set of circumstances. Teachers who are new to the profession or not familiar with alternatives to one dimensional testing should seek out teachers who have and are using a variety of strategies to assess children in their classroom; they should read about alternative assessment; they should watch teachers through video taped segments or visit classrooms where continuous assessment is practiced.

Observational skills are learned by observing. Teachers new to implementing the strategy must gain practice, skill and accuracy over time. When implementing portfolios as a strategy for assessment, teachers may want to depend on the collection of work samples to verify their observations. As they become more experienced the means by which data in the portfolios is collected will become more varied.

The early childhood profession has been and will continue to be accountable for the quality of educational programs children attend. As parents and children will be taking a more active role in curricular decisions, teachers will become decision *facilitators*. In this way accountability will be shared by all parties and not be viewed as an unknown that has driven decisions made by school policy makers and frightened some teachers into giving up appropriate teaching practices. *This is an example of the portfolio attitude.*

Today, policymakers, the media and the public all seem very concerned about education, especially early childhood education. President Bush and the nation's governors have set forth the readiness goal. Numerous states are providing new educational opportunities for three- and four-year-olds. Congress has appropriated more money for child care for poor families and for parents seeking job training with the intent of becoming self sufficient. The challenge is to see that these new programs and policies are developmentally appropriate and support the development of all children.

With the advent of school-based management programs, teachers are enjoying a new sense of empowerment and professionalism. They have the opportunity to reclaim their true responsibility. They can again become decision-makers or facilitators, planning appropriate learning experiences and assessment measures for children. The assessment portfolio can help teachers as they recreate their role in society and in the lives of children and families.

Since appropriate assessment is a collaborative process involving children, parents, teachers and the community, the portfolio method promotes a shared approach to making decisions which will affect the child's future and attitude toward learning. True partnerships are formed when parents and teachers work together in determining the best course of action for the young child. Portfolios serve as a departure point for parent and teacher communication to begin and to floorish. Again, *this is an example of the portfolio attitude.*

The time is right to expand the classroom horizon and broaden the child's canvas. The assessment portfolio represents an attitude that frees the teacher so that she may focus on the child and develop an intimate relationship with him — one that will remain long after the paintbrushes are put away.

References

Charlesworth, R. (1988). "Behind" before they start? Deciding how to deal with the risk of kindergarten "failure". *Young Children.* 44(3), 5-13.

Flesch, R. F. (1955). *Why Johnny can't read.* New York: Harper.

Jackson, P. (1968). *Life in the classroom.* New York: Holt, Rinehart and Winston.

Murray, F. (1986). *Necessity: The development component in reasoning.* Paper presented at the sixteen annual meeting, Jean Piaget Society, Philadelphia.

National Association of State Boards of Education. (1988). *Right from the start.* Alexandria, VA: Author.

Kindergarten Checklist

Student _____ Age _____ Birthdate _____

Teacher _____ School _____ Academic Year _____

Checklist Marking Symbols

Satisfactory (S)   The skill or behavior has become a natural part of your child's actions.

Improvement Needed (I)   The skill or behavior has not become a natural part of your child's actions at this time.

Slash Mark (/)   The skill or behavior has not been taught in the curriculum at this time.

Skill or behavior	Months		
	1	5	9
Social/Emotional			
Responds to rights and feelings of others			
Remains involved until task is completed			
Demonstrates adequate attention span			
Works and plays independently			
Works and plays in group			
Takes care of self physically			
Takes care of own/others' materials			
Accepts authority easily			
Exhibits a cooperative attitude			
Exhibits eagerness to learn			
Verbal, Cognitive and Linguistic			
Asks questions for information and word meaning			
Shares ideas freely			
Acquires new vocabulary through experiences			
Knows meaning of morning, afternoon, night			
Knows meaning of spring, summer, fall, winter			
Knows days of week in sequence			
Verbalizes full name, phone number, home address, age, and birthday			
Uses "more," "less," "same," "different" correctly			
Recites songs and short fingerplays and poems			
Describes items and actions in pictures			
Distinguishes between living and non-living things			
Engages in imitative play and uses appropriate vocabulary (role plays real-life situations)			
Names at least seven basic colors			
Speaks clearly			
Listens to poems and stories with interest			

Source: Hattiesburg, Mississippi Public School District

Kindergarten Checklist

Skill or behavior	Months		
	1	5	9
Exhibits curiosity about abstract words			
Understands left from right			
Can identify objects as to which is big, bigger, biggest, etc.			
Recognizes lower case letters (abcdefghijklmnopqrstuvwxyz)			
Recognizes upper case letters (ABCDEFGHIJKLMNOPQRSTUVWXYZ)			
Recognizes numerals to 20 (1 2 3 4 5 6 7 8 9 10 11 12 13 14 15 16 17 18 19 20)			
Recognizes likenesses and differences in letter sounds			
Enjoys looking at books			
Distinguishes rhyming words			
Distinguishes words beginning with same sound			
Knows left to right progression when looking at printed material			
Recognizes small number of printed words (labels, names, signs, etc.)			
Visual Perception			
Distinguishes differences among variety of shapes			
Identifies shapes in various sizes and positions			
Matches cut-out shapes of objects with actual objects			
Demonstrates understanding and usage of variety of spatial and positional terms			
Demonstrates ability to complete puzzles with more than 10 pieces			
Manipulates a variety of media to form objects			
Constructs objects with blocks and other types of building materials			
Throws and catches a ball with some accuracy and performs most body movements with coordination			
Pre-number and Number Concepts			
Exhibits understanding of one-to-one correspondence			
Sorts objects according to function, size, and shape			
Identifies circle, square, triangle, rectangle, straight line			
Duplicates sequential order of objects or pictures			
Understands purpose of calendar			
Understands purpose of clock			
Tells time by the hour			
Understands "before"' and "after"			
Understands purpose of thermometer			
Understands simple measurement techniques			
Joins sets of objects to sum of 10			
Separates sets out of 10			
Notes			

44

Activity Chart

Month ———————————————————————

Name ———————————————————————

	Sand & Water Play	Printing	Art	Music & Listening	Dramatic Play	Blocks	Math	Reading	Science	Language Arts	Social Studies
MON.											
TUES.											
WED.											
THURS.											
FRI.											
MON.											
TUES.											
WED.											
THURS.											
FRI.											
MON.											
TUES.											
WED.											
THURS.											
FRI.											
MON.											
TUES.											
WED.											
THURS.											
FRI.											
MON.											
TUES.											
WED.											
THURS.											
FRI.											

A check indicates the child completed the day's activity at the center.
Source: Esther Howard, Ph.D., Mississippi State University

Systematic Record

Directions: Each time a child comes to a center and completes an activity there, enter a tally mark in the appropriate space.

Child _____

Observer _____ Week of _____

Learning Center	Day					Total
	Mon.	Tues.	Wed.	Thurs.	Fri.	
Science center						
Book center						
Puzzle center						
Art center						
Writing center						

Source: Gloria Correro, Ph.D., Mississippi Department of Education

Anecdotal Record

Name of child _____ Date _____

Observer _____ Time _____

Setting _____

Incident: _____

_____

_____

_____

_____

Comments: _____

Is this report cross-filed?   Yes_____ No_____

Is supporting information available?   Yes___ No____

What is it?_____

Where is it?_____

Source: Gloria Correro, Ph.D., Mississippi Department of Education

---

Content and Key to Instrument Descriptors in Review Summary Tables

INSTRUMENT: *Instrument name, acronym, author(s), publication date and publisher.*

FOCUS: *Scope of content covered by the instrument.*

Broad:	Includes three or more of the following categories of abilities: Language, Speech, Cognition, Perception, Personal/Social, Perceptual-motor, Fine, Gross Motor Coordination
Academics:	Includes many, but primarily academic skills
Specific Areas:	Language, Literacy, Mathematics, Reading, Relational Concepts (see "Content" for specific skills in each area.)

AGE/GRADE: *Age or grade range covered by the instrument.*

ADM. TIME: *Time in minutes required for administration and initial scoring.*

FORMAT: Description of test in terms of type of response required, format and materials, categories are not mutually exclusive

Format:	Group or Individual Administration
	Multiple choice
	Paper & Pencil (child marks or writes the answer)
	Stimulus cards/easel
	Manipulatives (e.g., blocks, sorting chips)
Response Mode:	Teacher rating
	Parent response
	Observation of Child
	Oral (verbal)
	Pointing (implies multiple choice)
	Performance (fine/visual-motor: copy, build, write, etc)
	Motor (gross motor: hop, skip, jump, catch, etc.)

(Continued on next page)

Source: Northwest Regional Educational Laboratory, *Assessment in Early Education; A Consumer's Guide*

SCORES: *Types of scores available. No endorsement of the use of specific types of scores is implied here.*

Norm-referenced:	Percentile, Percentile Rank
	Age Equivalent / Grade Equivalent (Gr.Eq.)
	Standard Score
	Normal Curve Equivalent (NCE)
	Developmental "Age," "Language Age," etc.
	Quotient (Developmental, Language, etc.)
Criterion-referenced:	Mastery levels
	Raw score

CONTENT: *When the content covers a number of areas, the category name is used. When the content is more limited within a category, the specific areas are named.*

Basic facts:	colors (primary), letters, numbers, shapes
Language:	expressive, receptive vocabulary, fluency, syntax
Literacy:	print functions & conventions, reading symbols
Relational Concepts:	direction, position, size, quantity, order, time, categorization
Listening & Sequencing:	follows directions, remembers story sequences, main ideas
Cognitive:	problem solving, opposite analogies, memory, imitation
Perception:	auditory, visual discrimination
Mathematics:	count rote, with 1/1 correspondence, number skills
Motor:	fine motor (holding a pencil correctly, buttoning, etc)
	gross motor (hops, skips, throws)
	visual-motor (copies shapes, builds blocks)
Self:	knowledge of body parts (point or name)
	social/emotional (peer & teacher interactions, attention span, etc.)
	self help (buttoning, toilet, etc)
	information (name, age, address, phone, birthdate)

NORMS: *Ratings on norming studies (value judgement implied)*

None:	no normative information is given
Poor:	some information but limited applicability
Fair:	some standards of comparison (e.g., means of research sample)
Good:	norms based on good sized, representative sample, or lots of relevant information regarding appropriate populations for use
Excellent:	norms based on a representative, national sample and relevant information about applying norms or norm-referenced scores.

(Continued on next page)

RELIABILITY: *Reliability ratings (value judgement implied)*

       None: no reliability information is provided
       Poor: all reliability coefficients (r) below .70 or an important type of reliability was not examined
       Fair: at least one reported r is greater than .70; or r was greater than .80 but evidence was limited in applicability
       Good: total r is greater than .80; most subtests have r greater than .75
       Excellent: several kinds of reliability reported; total r is greater than .90; most subtest scores greater than .80

VALIDITY: *Validity ratings (value judgement implied)*

       None: no validity information is provided
       Poor: information is of very limited applicability
       Fair: most important aspects of were addressed but evidence was moderate or weak; or was strong but limited in applicability
       Good: consistent evidence of validity, or strong but limited evidence of the type of validity most appropriate for the intended test use
       Excellent: strong evidence and a base of research on the instrument

The following keys to ratings for norms, reliability and validity are provided with the summary tables.

NORMS: *Ratings on norming studies (value judgement implied)*

       None: no normative information is given
       Poor: some information but limited applicability
       Fair: some standards of comparison (e.g., means of research sample)
       Good: norms based on good sized, representative sample, or lots of other relevant information regarding appropriate populations for use
       Excellent: norms based on a representative, national sample and relevant information about applying norms or norm-referenced scores.

(Continued on next page)

RELIABILITY: *Reliability ratings (value judgement implied)*

              None: no reliability information is provided

              Poor: all reliability coefficients (r) below .70 or an important type of reliability was not examined

              Fair: at least one reported r is greater than .70; or r was greater than .80 but evidence was limited in applicability

              Good: total r is greater than .80; most subtests have r greater than .75

              Excellent: several kinds of reliability reported; total r is greater than .90; most subtest scores greater than .80

VALIDITY: *Validity ratings (value judgement implied)*

              None: no validity information is provided

              Poor: information is of very limited applicability

              Fair: most important aspects of were addressed but evidence was moderate or weak; or was strong but limited in applicability

              Good: consistent evidence of validity, or strong but limited evidence of the type of validity most appropriate for the intended test use

              Excellent: strong evidence and a base of research on the instrument

Summary of Instrument Characteristics
Screening Measures

INSTRUMENT	DESCRIPTION						TECHNICAL QUALITY			
	Focus	Ages Grades	Adm. Time	Format	Content	Scores	Norms	Reliability	Validity	Comment
Basic School Skills Inventory – Screening (BSSI-S) Hamill & Leigh, 1983 PRO-ED	Broad	Ages 4 - 6	5 - 10	Individually Adm Oral & Performance	Basic Facts Counting Speech Fine Motor	Standard Percentile	Poor	Fair Limited	Poor	
Battelle Developmental Inventory – Screening Test (BDI-S) DLM Teaching Resources	Broad	Ages 0 - 8	20 - 30 for ages 3 - 5	Individually Adm Perfor- mance, Oral, Motor, Pointing	Language Cognitive Motor Self	Multiple cutscore probability levels	Poor	None	Fair Limited	Heavily loaded with motor & personal/ social items No evidence for technical qualities of cutscores
Bracken Basic Concept Scale-Screening (BBCS-S) Bracken, 1984 The Psychological Corporation	Relational Concepts	Ages 5 - 7	15	Group Adm Paper & Pencil Multiple Choice	Survey of all Relational Concepts	Standard Percentile Stanine NCE	Fair	Fair	Poor Limited	The use of "concept age" score is not recommended
Brigance Preschool Screen Brigance, 1985 Curriculum Associates, Inc.	Broad	Ages 3 & 4	10 - 15	Individually Adm Spiral bound, Oral, Pointing, Performance	Colors, Motor Language Body Parts Personal data	Raw scores for group ranking	None	None	Content Fair Screen- ing Poor	Parent & Teacher Rating Forms available Not validated for screening
Brigance K & 1 Screen Brigance, 1982 Curriculum Associates, Inc.	Broad	Grades K & 1	10 - 15	Individually Adm Spiral bound, Oral, Pointing, Performance	Basic Facts Language Mathematics Motor	Raw scores for group ranking	None	None	Good Limited	Parent & Teacher Rating Forms available Author has not validated this test for screening
The Communication Screen Striffler & Willig, 1981 (TCS) Communication Skill Builders	Language	Ages 2, 10 to 5, 9	2 - 5	Individually Adm Stimulus card, Oral & Perform. Observations	Language Cognitive	Pass Suspect Fail	Prelimi- nary Limited	Fair Limited	Fair Limited	Developed by clinicians Needs more evidence of technical quality, smaller age groups for scoring
Denver Developmental Screening Tes (DDST) Frankenburg it al., 1975 LA-DOCA Project & Publishing Fndtn.	Broad	Ages 0 - 6	20	Individually Adm Manipulatives Motor, Oral Performance	Self Fine Motor Language Gross Motor	Cutscores	Poor Dated	Fair Limited	Fair	Conservative test, errs on the side of underreferrals

Source: Northwest Regional Educational Laboratory, *Assessment in Early Education; A Consumer's Guide*

Summary of Instrument Characteristics
Screening Measures, cont.

INSTRUMENT	DESCRIPTION						TECHNICAL QUALITY			
	Focus	Ages Grades	Adm. Time	Format	Content	Scores	Norms	Reliability	Validity	Comment
Developmental Activities Screening Inventory II Fewell & Langley, 1984 (DASI II) PRO-ED	Primarily Academics	Ages 0 - 5	Untimed	Individually Adm Pointing Performance few oral	Colors Classify Visual Motor Memory Spatial Reltnsr	Developm. Age & Quotient	None	None	Poor	
Developmental Indicators for the Assessment of Learning-Revised (DIAL-R) Childcraft Education Corp.	Broad	Ages 4 - 6	5 - 10	Individually Adm Oral & Performance	Basic Facts Counting Speech Fine Motor	Standard Percentile	Fair	Fair Limited	Fair	
Early Identification Screening Program (EISP) Baltimore City Public Schools, 1982 Modern Curriculum Press	Academics	Grades K & 1	20	Individually Adm Performance Oral	Perception Colors (name) Shapes Visual Motor	Total raw score	None	Good	Fair	
Early Screening Inventory (ESI) Meisels & Wiske, 1983 Teachers College Press	Broad	Ages 4 - 6	15 - 20	Individually Adm Performance Motor & Oral	Cognitive Counting Language Motor	Cutscores: OK Rescreen Refer	Fair	Good Limited	Good	Extensive new norm study underway includes 3-year-olds
Florida Kindergarten Screening Battery (FKSB) Satz & Fletcher, 1982 Psychological Assessmt Resources	Language Perception	Grade K	20	Individually Adm Oral, Performance	Vocabulary Visual Motor Perception Alphabet	Individual test scores are weighted	Fair	Fair	Fair	Impressive longitudinal validity studies but of limited generalizability
Fluharty Preschool Speech and Language Screening Test Fluharty, 1978 DLM Teaching Resources	Language	Ages 2 - 6	6	Individually Adm Picture cards Oral Pointing	Vocabulary Articulation Comprehension Repetition	Cutscores for each subtest	Good	Good Limited	Unclear	Specific instructions on how to make allow-ances for Black dialect Cutscore develop. unclear
Kindergarten Language Screening Test (KLST) Gauthier & Madison, 1983 PRO-ED	Language	Grade K	10	Individually Adm Oral	Basic Facts Language Self Follow Direction	Total raw score	Fair Limited	Fair Limited	Good	Measures a broad variety of language skills

Summary of Instrument Characteristics
Screening Measures, cont.

INSTRUMENT	DESCRIPTION						TECHNICAL QUALITY			
	Focus	Ages Grades	Adm. Time	Format	Content	Scores	Norms	Reliability	Validity	Comment
McCarthy Screening Test (MST) McCarthy, 1978 The Psychological Corporation	Broad	Ages 4 - 6 1/2	20	Individually Adm Manipula- tive Motor, Oral Performance	Motor Cognitive Language Mathematics	Pass/Fail by subtest Cutscores: # failed	Good Dated	Fair Limited	Good Limited	Developed from MSCA No independent norms validity or reliability
Miller Assessment for Preschoolers (MAP) Miller, 1984 The Psychological Corporation	Broad	Ages 2,9 - 5,8	25 - 35	Individually Adm Motor Performance Oral	Broad range of Motor and Language Skills	Percentile cutscores	Excel- lent	Good	Good	Training video available Supplemental behavior observations
Mullen Scales of Early Learning (MSEL) Mullen, 1984 T.O.T.A.L. Child, Inc.	Broad	Ages 1,3 - 5,8	35 - 45	Individually Adm Manipulatives Picture Books Oral & Perform.	Perception Language Cognitive Visual Motor	Age scores T-scores	Good	Good	Good Limited	Test materials include colorful toys attractive to children
Pediatric Examination of Educational Readiness (PEER) Levine & Schneider, 1982 Educators Publishing Service	Broad	Ages 4 - 6	60	Individually Adm Performance Oral, Motor	Language Basic Facts Motor Orientation	Concern Level cutscores	Fair	Fair Limited	Good Limited	Designed for medical setting or interdiscipli- nary screening
Preschool Development Inventory (PDI) Ireton, 1984 Behavior Science Systems	Primarily Academics	Ages 3 -5 1/2	25	Individually Adm Parental rating Yes/No format	Language Motor Self, Social Problem behav.	cutscores	Fair Limited	None	Poor Limited	
Screening for Related Early Educational Needs (SCREEN) Hresko et al., 1988 PRO-ED	Academics	Ages 3 - 7	15 - 40	Individually Adm Pointing, Oral Performance	Language Reading Writing Mathematics	Standard Percentile	Good	after age 6 Good Limited	Fair	Little evidence of reliability and validity is poor for the 3-5 age range
SEARCH Silver & Hagin, (1981) Walker Educational Book Corp.	Perception	Ages 5,3 to 6,8	20	Individually Adm Manipulatives Performance Oral, Motor	Perception Perceptual/ Motor, Memory Articulation	Ability Profile Stanines Cutscores	Fair Dated (1973)	Fair Limited	Fair Limited	Multiethnic content depiction

Summary of Instrument Characteristics
Mastery of Readiness Concepts

INSTRUMENT	DESCRIPTION						TECHNICAL QUALITY			
	Focus	Ages Grades	Adm. Time	Format	Content	Scores	Norms	Reliability	Validity	Comment
Analysis of Readiness Skills Rodriguez, Vogler & Wilson, 1972 The Riverside Publishing Company	Academics (Limited)	Grade K	30 - 40	Individualy or Group/Adm Paper & Pencil Multiple Choice	Letter Discrim & Naming Number names & Counting	Percentile	Poor Dated	Poor Limited	Poor Limited	Traditional concept of readiness skills
Basic School Skills Inventory - Diagnostic (BSSI-D) Hammill & Leigh, 1983 PRO-ED	Broad	Ages 4 - 6	20 - 30	Individually Adm Teacher ratings Performance Oral	Language Literacy Mathematics Self/behavior	Percentile Standard	Fair	Fair	Poor	
Boehm Test of Basic Concepts - Revised (Boehm-R) Boehm, 1986 The Psychological Corporation	Relational Concepts	Grades K 1-2	30	Group Adm Paper & Pencil	All areas of Relational Concepts	Total raw score Percentile	Excel- lent	Grade K Good Overall Fair	Grade K Excel- lent Overall Good	Class record form - Key Parent/teacher Conference Report form available
Boehm Test of Basic Concepts - Preschool Version (Boehm) Boehm, 1986 The Psychological Corporation	Relational Concepts	Ages 3 - 5	10 - 15	Individually Adm Paper & Pencil	All areas of Relational Concepts	Total raw score Percentile	Fair	Good Limited	Good Limited	Class record form - Key Parent/teacher Conference Report form available
Bracken Basic Concept Scale - Diagnostic (BBCS-D) Bracken, 1984 The Psychological Corporation	Relational Concepts	Ages 2 1/2 to 8	20 - 30	Individually Adm Multiple Choice Pointing or Oral	All areas of Relational Concepts	Standard Percentile Stanines NCE	Fair	Fair	good	Exhaustive set of 258 concepts The use of "concept age" score is not recommended
CIRCUS ITS, 1972, 1979 CTB/McGraw-Hill	Academics	Grades Pre-K K & 1	30 per subtest	Group Adm Paper & Pencil Multiple choice	Perception Mathematics Language Cognition	Standard Percentile Stanine	Excel- lent	Good	Good Limited	Many subtests can be used separately or in groups; Teacher Observation Instrument available
Cognitive Skills Assessment Battery (CSAB) Boehm & Slater, 1981 Teachers	Academics	Ages Pre-K & K	20 - 25	Individually Adm Stim. Card Easel Oral, Perform. Written	Concepts Perception Cognition Self	% Pass by item Means for area	Fair	Fair Limited	Fair	Fall & spring norms by SES level Behavior rating scale available

Summary of Instrument Characteristics
Mastery of Readiness Concepts, cont.

INSTRUMENT	DESCRIPTION						TECHNICAL QUALITY			
	Focus	Ages Grades	Adm. Time	Format	Content	Scores	Norms	Reliability	Validity	Comment
Gesell Preschool Test Haines, Ames & Gillespie, 1980 Programs for Education, Inc.	Broad	Ages 2 1/2 - 6	30 - 45	Individually Adm Manipulatives Oral & Performance	Self Language Visual Motor	Age based success level by item	Poor Limited	None	Poor Limited	Reliability and validity have not been established
Gesell School Readiness Test aka School Readiness Screening Test (SRST), 1978 Programs for Education, Inc.	Broad	Ages 4 1/2 - 9 4 1/2 - 5	20 - 30	Individually Adm Manipulatives Performance Oral	Self Language Visual Motor	Age based success levels	Poor Limited Dated	None	Poor Limited	Clinical approach to scoring requires extensive training
The Lollipop Test Chew, 1981, 1989 Humanics LTD	Academics	Grades Pre-K & K	15 - 20	Individually Adm Pointing, Oral Copying	Basic Facts Relt.Concepts Copy Shapes Math & Writing	Raw Scores Suggested Mastery Levels	Fair	Fair	Good	Attractively packaged Child & examiner friendly
Metropolitan Readiness Tests - Fifth Edition (MRT) Nurss & MacGauvan, 1986 The Psychological Corporation	Academics	Grades Pre-K K & 1	80 - 95	Group Adm Paper & Pencil Multiple Choice Performance	Language Literacy Perception Mathematics	Raw Score Percentile Stanine Mast. levels	Excel- lent	Good	Good	Instructional Materials Parent/teacher Conference Report forms Behavior checklists
Preschool Inventory (PI) Caldwell, 1970 CTB/McGraw-Hill	Academics	Ages 3 - 6	15	Individually Adm Manipulatives Oral Motor Performance	Self Language Basic Facts Copy Forms	Percentile % Pass by item	Fair Dated Limited	Fair Limited	Fair	Clear SES differences Norm group all Head Start children available
School Readiness Survey - Jordan & Massey, 1976 (SRS) Consulting Psychologists Press	Academics	Grades Pre-K	Untimed	Individually Adm by the Parent Multiple Choice Pointing, Oral	Basic Facts Perception Cognitive Vocab. & Self	Readiness Levels	Fair Dated	Fair	Fair	Effective communication device to discuss school readiness with parents
Tests of Basic Experiences Second Edition (TOBE 2) Moss, 1979 CTB/McGraw-Hill	Academics	Grades Pre-K K & 1	160 40 per subtest	Group Adm Paper & Pencil Multiple Choice	Language Mathematics Science Social Studies	Standard Percentile Stanines NCE	Excel- lent	Good Limited	Fair Limited	Optional 1 item/page books. Fall, winter, spring norms Public & Catholic norms Practice Test

Summary of Instrument Characteristics
Mastery of Readiness Concepts, cont.

INSTRUMENT	DESCRIPTION						TECHNICAL QUALITY			
	Focus	Ages Grades	Adm. Time	Format	Content	Scores	Norms	Reliability	Validity	Comment
Test of Early Language Development (TELD) Hresko, Reid & Hammill 1981 PRO-ED	Language	Ages 3 - 7	15 - 20	Individually Adm Stimulus cards Oral Pointing	Expressive Receptive Vocabulary Syntax	Percentile Lang Quot Lang Age.	Fair Limited	Excellent	Good	Well written, helpful manual
Test of Early Mathematics Ability (TEMA) Ginsburg & Baroody, 1983 PRO-ED	Mathematics	Ages 4 - 8+	20	IndividuallyAdm Stimulus cards Manipulatives Oral, Perform.	Quantitative Concepts Counting Calculation	Percentile Math Quot Math Age.	Fair Limited	Good Limited	Fair	New version coming in 1989 This version has limited utility for pre-K or beg. K
Test of Early Reading Ability (TERA) Reid, Hresko & Hammill, 1981 PRO-ED	Reading	Ages 4 - 8+	15 - 20	Individually Adm Stimulus cards Oral, Pointing	Wide range of Early Literacy Skills	Percentile Standard Lang Age.	Good	Excellent	Fair Limited	All new version for 1989 This version difficult below age 6
Test of Early Written Language (TEWL) Hresko, 1988 PRO-ED	Literacy	Ages 3-8	10 - 30	Individually Adm Stimulus cards Writing, Oral, Pointing	Range of Early Literacy Skills	Percentile Standard	Fair Limited Info	Good Limited	Poor Limited	Administration instructions tend to hurry child Norms do not account for experiential differences
Test of Language Development - Primary (TOLD-2 Primary) Hresko, Reid & Hammill 1981 PRO-ED	Language	Ages 4 - 8+	30 - 60	Individually Adm Stimulus cards Oral, Pointing	Expressive Receptive Vocabulary Syntax	Percentile Standard Lang Quot. T- z- NCE	Excellent	Excellent	Good	Well written, helpful manual

Other Resources

For more information about appropriate assessment, contact one of these associations. Many of these associations sponsor conferences and publish journals and other publications, through which teachers, administrators and parents can learn more about helping young children learn.

Southern Association on Children Under Six (SACUS)
P.O. Box 5403
Little Rock, AR 72215-5403

Association for Early Childhood Education International (ACEI)
11141 Georgia Ave., Suite 200
Wheaton, MD 20902

FairTest/National Center for Fair and Open Testing
342 Broadway
Cambridge, MA 02139-1802

National Association for the Education of Young Children
1834 Connecticut Ave., N.W.
Washington, DC 20009

National Association of Early Childhood Specialists in State Departments of Education
Chalmer Moore, President
Illinois State Board of Education
100 N. First Street, S-100
Springfield, Illinois 62777

National Association of Elementary School Principals
1615 Duke Street
Alexandria, VA 22314

National Association of State Boards of Education
1012 Cameron Street
Alexandria, VA 22314

National Black Child Development Institute
1463 Rhode Island Ave., N.W.
Washington, DC 20005

National Head Start Association
1309 King St., Suite 200
Alexandria, VA 22314

Southern Regional Education Board
592 10th St., N.W.
Atlanta, GA 30318-5790

Index

Cathy Grace, Ed.D., coordinated the establishment of public kindergarten in the State of Mississippi in 1983-86. She has been a first grade teacher and an assistant professor of early childhood education at Mississippi Valley State University and the University of Southern Mississippi. She holds a doctorate in education from the University of Mississippi. A native of Arkansas, she is the executive director of the Southern Association on Children Under Six.

Elizabeth F. Shores is publications editor for the Southern Association on Children Under Six. She has worked as a writer and editor in the South for 13 years. She is a native of Alabama and holds a B.A. in American Civilization from Boston University.

About SACUS

Persons who want to learn more about appropriate testing, instruction and curriculum for young children may want to join the Southern Association on Children Under Six (SACUS). SACUS publishes a quarterly journal, *Dimensions*, that contains timely articles about early childhood education. SACUS also produces a wide variety of other educational materials and sponsors many training opportunities for teachers and caregivers. For more information, write:

Southern Association on Children Under Six (SACUS)
P.O. Box 5403
Little Rock, AR 72215-5403